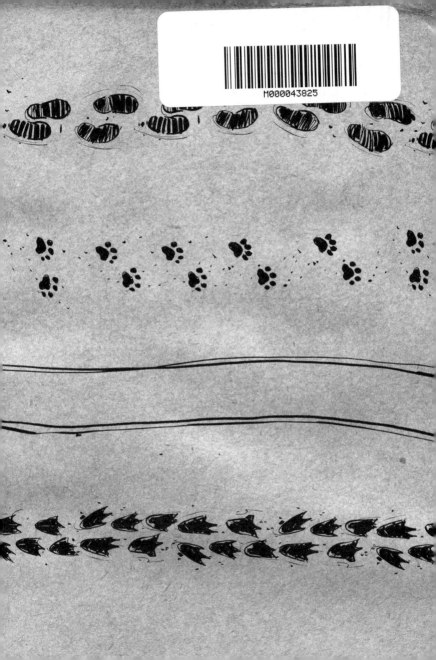

The Girl,
the Penguin,
the Home-schooling
& the Gin.

Guy: This book is dedicated to the real girl, Verity, the real penguin Boo-Boo and the very best drinker of gin, Alexandra.

W.R. Foster: This one's for Velma, the finest Sheila you could ever hope to raise a glass with. Good on ya doll!

The Girl, the Penguin, the Home-schooling & the Gin.

- A PARODY -

Guy Adams & W. R. Foster

J̃B

Hello!

If you're anything like us then you're feeling jaded, unfit and sore. The Internet is screaming. You know you should cut down on the drink, and the junk food and the drink and the drink and the junk food and the drink and oh God but I'm dancing to the music in the supermarket and now I'm going for a refreshing nap in the freezer and the peas are like crunchy love pillows and how I wish I could just stay here forever pushing ice creams, sweet creamy chill parcels, into my quivering, crying face.

If you're anything like us.

Don't worry, help is at hand. If recent publishing trends have shown us anything, it's that the one way to feel better about ourselves is to look at pretty pictures of animals while they say things that sound useful but — and this is the important bit — probably aren't.

Because it's all been ever so thinky of late hasn't it? Really brain chewy. And, given a choice, who would want challenging and life altering guidance from a therapist if the alternative was a pithy comment about sunsets from a smiling otter?

We don't have otters. But we do have penguins. Everybody loves penguins. And cats. And dogs on wheels. Hopefully.

So kick back and relax, sure in the knowledge that we have things covered in the anthropomorphic advice-dosing department.

Please don't worry, nothing's going to make you question yourself. Much. I write things, he draws things—who the hell are we to tell you you're doing it wrong? We frequently email each other to congratulate ourselves on having woken up during daylight. In our own clothes. Under a roof. Without blood all over us.

We hope reading this book encourages you to live however you want to and to extend that same courtesy to others. Be they penguins, cats, dogs on wheels or, you know, if you absolutely must, other humans.

The only essential advice that occurs to us:

Don't eat anything that's still moving.
Don't run with scissors.
Be nice.

Yours,

G.   W.R.

The Writer, the Artist and the nervous breakdowns.

"Now Then!"

"You talk?!"

"I talk?" said the penguin, "So what? Jesus H Osman! Small stuff! What have you been doing with your frigging life that you think talking penguins is news?"

"You have a salty tongue," said the girl.

"I'm a penguin, pickle, I'm salty from tit to toe."

"Oopla!"
the penguin shouted.
"What does that mean?"
asked the girl.

"No idea," admitted the penguin,
"but it makes you feel good if you
shout it. I'll teach you some others."

"The thing with words," said the penguin, "is that people spend too much time learning them and not enough enjoying them. It's always worth inventing a few or borrowing ones people don't use anymore — like those little braces that keep your socks up — and taking them for a spin."

Calabash!

Zim! Zim!

Pompadello!

Frustbitz!

Bitterzair!

"Are those the sort of words your
mummy and daddy shout?" asked
the penguin. "When they're grumped
up and frazzled?"

"No," said the girl,
"they shout very different things."

Words my parents shout:

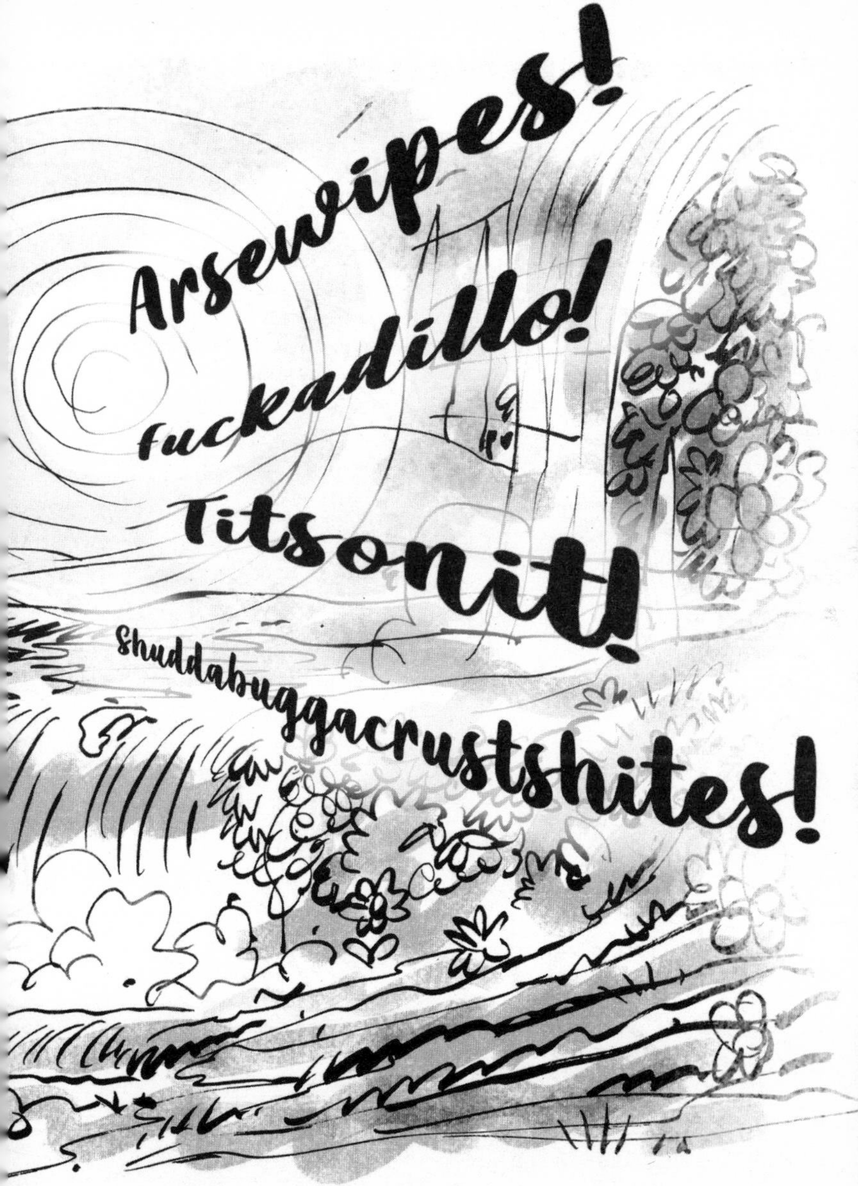
Arsewipes!
Fuckadillo!
Titsonit!
Shuddabuggacrustshites!

"Yippee," said the penguin, "it's the Boris Johnson of the animal world. A puffy-bonced sociopath that thinks it's clever."

"A species that loves necrophilia really shouldn't be throwing shade," said the cat.

"Hey," said the penguin, "cold or warm,
don't diss the cloacal kiss!"

"Take a look at those two," said the penguin. "I'd rather eat vegan fish sticks than be seen within six foot of 'em."

"Hello Mommy and Daddy,"

Look at them.

Nothing a mortician couldn't fix.

"WHAT DOESN'T KILL YOU
MAKES YOU STRONGER,"

...said someone who has never viewed
paracetamol as an essential vitamin.

...said someone who has never, at a point
of complete and utter washing-up crisis,
eaten cereal out of a dripping carrier bag.

...said someone who has never considered
park bins a valid food source.

"Responsibility finds a way..."

"Work can be play with a positive mind!"

"Find the path through life
that is yours and yours alone."

"Find adventure in the everyday business of life."

"To get the things you want in life requires patience, resilience and **a killer left hook.**"

"The road to happiness begins on a path of self-love."

Self-Love Regime:

10.00 CROISSANTS/BREAKFAST, WINE
10.30 FIRST NAP
12.00 LUNCH
13.00 EXERCISE
13.15 SECOND NAP
15.00 BISCUIT AND A FRISKY FIDDLE
15.10 COCKTAIL HOUR
16.00 THIRD NAP
17.00 COCKTAIL HOUR (CONT.)
19.00 DIN-DINS
20.00 FREE TIME

"Charge yourself."

A fire with no heat warms nobody.

A car with no petrol drives nowhere.

A sex toy with no batteries fizzes no fannies.

"On this adventure called life, we must choose our fellow travellers carefully."

Because most people will make your tits itch and you've enough on your plate without adding 'quicklime a corpse'.

"A day spent with you is an adventure,
so let me finish it breathless."

"Your real friends never judge you."

"Do you think mommy and daddy will ever get over it?" asked the girl.

"Well," said the penguin, "they survived Bowie dying, just, so I reckon they can get over anything."

Foster,
You old lush.
Feeling too hung-
-over to come
up with a joke
for page 48.
Any ideas?
Gx
Sod it, we'll
just drop a blank
page in.
The original did
that all the time.
Wxx

"Hi! I'm a Dog on Wheels!"

If there's anything better than wheels for feet
and stuffing for brains then buy me a
one - way ticket to Don't-want-to-knowsville!"

"I'm a Dog on Wheels," said the Dog on Wheels
"and I'm just full of advice."

1. It's always darkest when it's, like, really dark.

2. There's no such thing as accidents, just bad aim

3. Everything will be alright in the end, and
if it's not alright then it's the end so who cares?

"Well," said the penguin,
"I do hope someone here
is going to slip Tigger a bromide."

"Be Weird."

"Never be ashamed to ask for help.
Some things in life need more hands,
like bathing a toddler,
getting the week's wine delivery in
or committing any of the
really exciting murders."

"We all need a reason to keep going," said the girl. "What's yours?"

"Blind, idiotic devotion," said the cat.

Trending on Twitter for all the wrong reasons," said the penguin.

"The moist, tasty beauty of self-cleaning," said the Dog on Wheels.

"The hardest person to forgive is yourself."

"...especially if you've just eaten
an entire pack of chocolate biscuits as breakfast.
Again."

"All things pass..."

Including:

Hangovers,

Wind,

Prison sentences,

Shame.

Don't worry if you feel frightened...

All sane people are frightened.

Because someone had to go and invent ...

Wasps, vicious zips, chip pan fires...

There's something terrifying for everyone:

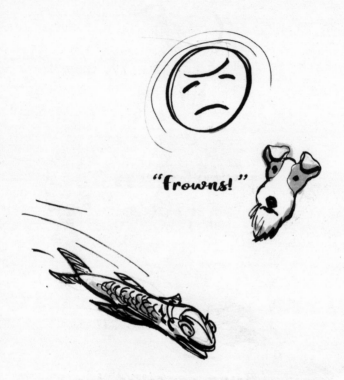

"Frowns!"

"Attack Herring."

"Ice cream allergy."

"Being cancelled due
to my mouse habit ..."

"Long division!"

"Mask sneeze!"

"Coughing people!"

"Working for Wetherspoons!"

" Back off, germ sacks! "

" Burn the receipt..."

And, through it all,
what did we learn?

There is no fart louder
than a Zoom meeting fart.

We can choose how we respond
to those who upset us.

No pain—no gain!

There is no greater gift
than teaching,
To pass on the vital lessons

we have learned in life...
The riches of our wisdom.

like long division,
grammar that nobody's
ever heard of
and the essential, impeccable
truth that is the boiling point
of mercury.

And that our definition of success
is a constantly moving thing.

"What do you think success is...?"

"To write a self-help book."

In which case, let us tell you
all you need to know:

However hard it is...

However endless it seems ...

However impossible it feels ...

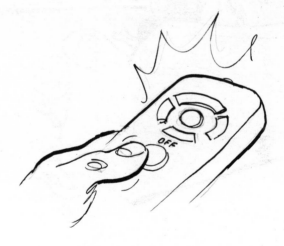

The secret to life is this:

We muddle through.

We get by.

#BOYCOTT EVERYTHING
#GO GREEN-ISH!
#KEEP 2 METRES
#NO MORE
ANTIFA RULE
OPEN BORDERS
#UNVACCINATED
REFUGEES
BUILD BACK
CLAP FOR THE NHS
#NOT MY PROBLEM
BUILD BRIDGES--- NOT
EAT THE RICH!
#BOO THE KNEE
RISE

And, remember,
however difficult it is to
believe some days...

"We are all heroes . . ."

The End

GUY ADAMS WOULD LIKE TO THANK . . .

The Artist, naturally. The Editor, obviously.

Alexandra, endlessly. Verity, bouncingly.
Nana and Grandpapa, effusively.
Messrs Whyte and Mackay, frequently.

W.R. FOSTER WOULD LIKE TO THANK . . .

The Writer, unnaturally. The Editor, apparently.

Frankie Howerd, titteringly. Thelonious Monk, specifically.
Trappist Monks, generally. Iggy Pop, enormously.
Morrissey, lovingly. Louise Brooks, silently. Frank Sinatra, swingingly.
Lou Reed, iconically. Bob Dylan, belatedly. Prince, funkily.
Rambling Syd Rumpo, waywardly.
Spike Milligan, crazily. Old Mother Riley, nostalgically.
Joey, Johnny, Dee-Dee and Tommy, collectively.
Her majesty the Queen, obediently.
Benny Hill, cheekily. Paul Newman, handsomely.
John, Paul, George and Ringo, hysterically.
Ronald Searle, endlessly. Vladimir Nabakov, secretly.
William and Ralph Foster, eponymously.

And to Charlie Mackesy,
without whom 2020 would have been
far less tolerable and 2021
would have been far less busy.

FIRST PUBLISHED IN THE UK BY JOHN BLAKE PUBLISHING
AN IMPRINT OF BONNIER BOOKS UK
4TH FLOOR, VICTORIA HOUSE
BLOOMSBURY SQUARE,
LONDON, WC1B 4DA
ENGLAND

OWNED BY BONNIER BOOKS
SVEAVÄGEN 56, STOCKHOLM, SWEDEN

WWW.FACEBOOK.COM/JOHNBLAKEBOOKS
TWITTER.COM/JBLAKEBOOKS

FIRST PUBLISHED IN HARDBACK IN 2021

ISBN: 978-1-78946-568-6
EBOOK: 978-1-78946-588-4

BRITISH LIBRARY CATALOGUING-IN-PUBLICATION DATA:

A CATALOGUE RECORD FOR THIS BOOK IS AVAILABLE FROM THE BRITISH LIBRARY.

TYPESETTING BY WWW.ENVYDESIGN.CO.UK
PRINTED AND BOUND IN GREAT BRITAIN BY CLAYS LTD, ELCOGRAF S.P.A.

1 3 5 7 9 10 8 6 4 2

JOHN BLAKE PUBLISHING IS AN IMPRINT OF BONNIER BOOKS UK
WWW.BONNIERBOOKS.CO.UK

MIX
Paper from
responsible sources
FSC® C018072
www.fsc.org

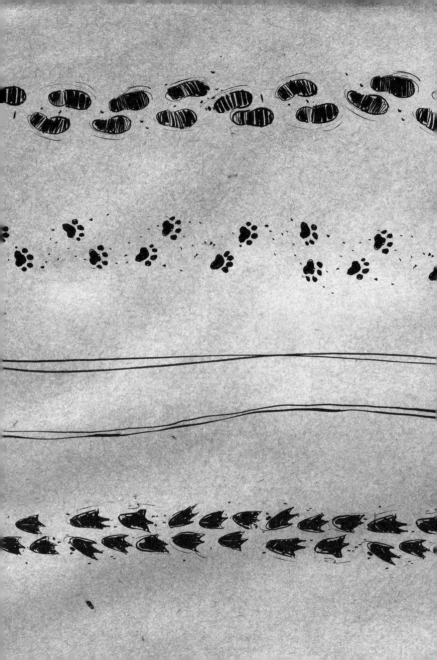